The Lemon Squeeze

The Lemon Squeeze is your STEP BY STEP GUIDE of what to do to get the next job and what to do to take care of yourself both "MENTALLY AND PHYSICALLY" while you FIGHT to move forward. Make no mistake it is going to be the FIGHT OF YOUR LIFE. When life throws you LEMONS!!! This is what to do to make LEMONAID!!

There is much to consider when finding your next job. You have to be ready to take care of yourself and the stress that can destroy you or at the very less send you into a state of depression. These issues are real and we are going to help you prepare for this world changing event and Win the new JOB!!!

You must understand how to take care of yourself-Mentally, Physically and Financially. To be successful you must take care of you!!

You are in the world's biggest competition for someone to pick you over someone else. You must not leave any opportunity unturned and we have the QUICK recipe to get you organized and employers knowing you are a great choice: We have prepared the Traditional Job Seek Tools and we have THE PLAN to use the new exciting "Social Networking Tools" to streamline and maximize all avenues to find your new life!! All while taking care of YOU!

This is the beginning of taking care of your family, getting your self-respect back and reclaiming a way to pay for your lifestyle.

In today's world, you have to be aware of what to do to win a job. You have to quickly develop the tools, know how the Human Resource decision makers are using social networking and how you must use social networking to maximize your opportunity to find the next job.

We have the Traditional Job Search Tools-Cover letter, resume and references. We have the folders organized and Sample documents that are the "CURRENT RESUME fashion style" ready for you to use, just fill in the blanks. This is what Human Resource (HR) Decision Makers Demand!

First, you must realize that whatever caused this situation you will overcome it, yes you will WIN!!

Let's get stated with the "Bailey Plan", now write your last name here "_____ Plan" because from here on out it is all about you. I got your back, you will WIN, YOU ARE A WINNER!!

I have been a professional executive for over 30 years. I have worked for 10 companies. I changed jobs for career advancement 5 times, 3 companies closed and laid off 2 times (both companies sold/closed).

But every time I was handed LEMONS and had to find a new job, I have been successful. I have the plan and if GOD has shown me this plan I believe it is for me to share it for YOUR success!!!

Index

Introduction
Index

g. Hot Leads Folder-Potential Job Contacts/Interview tracking list

h. Job Description Folder-The employer's description of what they want. We use this blueprint to highlight employer's hot buttons in our Resume and Cover Letter.

II. Equipment and Folder Development you will need: Computer, Flash   Drive and a "New" Email Account:

1. Resume Folder Development
2. Cover Letter Folder Development
3. Application Folder Development
4. Reference Folder Development
5. Job Description Folder Development

III. Let's Get Started:

A. The Resume-Complete the "Master Information Sheet".

B. Complete Sample Cover Letters-See Cover Letter Folder.

C. Complete References-See "Reference Folder"

IV. Battle Ground/Getting the Word Out

A. Internet Job Search Set up and DANGER!!

1. Using the User Name/Password Spreadsheet
2. Testing the User Name and Password
3. Upload Cover letter, Resume and References

B. Corporate Job Search Strategy

1. Setting Up The Corporate Job Searches:
This is your step by step guide to using the internet to get and stay on the corporate scene. Most of all you will stay in the know on what positions are available as soon as they are available. Remember first come, first served!

C. Our Internet Strategy
We have all our workers set up to generate new leads, track the application process and we know when to make direct contact.

V. Targeting-Getting the Word Out-Part II

   1. How To Target Corporations and Opportunities
   2. List Corporations
   3. Register
   4. Set Up Search Engines
   5. DANGER: Traps to "AVOID"

VI.   Government Job-Getting the Word Out-Part III
      A. How to start and what to do on Local, State, County and Federal Government Employment Web Sites.

VII.   Finances-What to do Immediately, Second and Third-YOU WILL MAKE IT!!
       Part 1-What to do first (We have your plan), Part 1-The Basics

Part 2-Time Frame for making financial decisions, first 30 Day, first 60 days, etc.

Part 3-How to handle your Family, Friends and Lovers

    1. This is for your "Significant Other"-How to help your unemployed lover!

Part 4-Physical: You must keep your physical body together!!

Supporting Documents Attached-Example of all documents you need is included! All folders and documents are already set up on line-lbailey989@icloud.com

I. MENTAL:

a. Why did this happen to me: SEE MENTAL REPAIR

b. Reality Check- You need another job:

You don't have a job-You are upset, fearful at what you are going to do, wondering how did this happen to me, the company treated me horrible, what did I do wrong, I am so ashamed and again what am I going to do!! ☹

First of all, write this out on paper, get it out of your brain so you can stop wasting time thinking about it!! Make sure you end with now I am moving forward there is nothing else to do. You do not want to hurt yourself (You Love You and Your Family Needs you). You will be a real life lesson on when life throws you Lemons-You must make LEMONADE!!! (See Mental Repair –Why Did This Happen to Me- workout sheet)

You don't want to bail on life by committing a revenge crime like murdering the horrible former boss that fired you or laid you off, stealing company secrets or property, threatening co-workers or even writing to co-workers-IT IS TIME TO MOVE ON AND YOU ARE MOVING TO THE NEXT GREAT ADVENTURE OF YOUR LIFE!!

It is time to put on your Big Boy Pants and Move Forward. Treat yourself well; pull your team together (family, friends and network of professional contacts-See Team List Folder). Let "YOUR TEAM" know what is going on-tell them you need everyone to stay positive. Take a deep breath and now let's make our first move to a better life than you have right now. Don't focus on the past only the FUTURE!! FUTURE! GOD will lead you to your greatness!

c. Moving Forward:

YOU are a valuable asset. The world only has one of you and now you are telling the world they can share your magnificence.

You will feel immediately better once you make the move forward plan and set strict due dates for yourself, it will keep you focused!! But let's have some joy!! We listen to ONLY POSITIVE MUSIC AND TELEVISION-NOTHING NEGATIVE, WE LOOK AT ONLY POSITIVE ARTICLES/NOTHING SAD AND YOU READ MOTIVING INFORMATION (Web Site with positive information-i.e. Thought of the Day, Brandon's Word Of Your Day, etc.).

In summary, let's put the game show channel on television; listen to music you like or a book on tape. Set a positive environment to enjoy life!! Let's make this experience enjoyable, this is your life and you must make yourself have joy. Kiss your loved ones, hug them, pick them up from school or go to functions you could never attend (just make sure you are working 6 to 8 hours a day). Make sure you are taking Saturday or Sunday off to take a mental break, you must find joy!

d. Equipment and set up you will need

You will need to have access to the following equipment and set up folders to organize the journey:
1. Computer
2. Folder Set Up
   a. Resume Folder
   b. Cover Letter Folder
   c. Application Folder
   d. Reference Folder
   e. Team List
   f. Username/Password Folder
   g. Hot Leads Folder
   h. Job Description Folder

II.   Equipment and Folder Development you will need:

You need to use a computer or paper files (I highly recommend a computer). Hopefully you have a computer at home. If you do not have a computer, plan to go to the library daily and use the free computers. This is your new job.

You must get a flash drive that you will use to store all information associated with the" ___ (Your Name) ___ Plan Moving Forward to my Greatness!"

        a. On the flash drive set up the following folders:
           1. Resume
           2. Cover Letter
           3. Application
           4. References
           5. Job Description

You must get a New Email Account: I used lbailey@icloud.com to set up a new email account. Select an account that has a conservative name Leesmith123@ ___ .com. You will only use this email for job correspondence. Everything that shows up on this email account relates to your future job.

1. Resume:

–Open the Resume Folder. (See "Resume" Folder) The Resume Folder set up all information needed to formulate a resume. See Current Human Resources (HR) desired resume format. Don't think the resume style you used 10 or 5 years ago is in VOUGE or a current style. Remember the HR department is looking for <u>current</u>, in the know, superstars. See Resume Format-(make sure to "SAVE AS" your working copy so you don't lose the RESUME FORMAT QUESTIONS) Located in the Resume Folder, you need to read the resume, answer questions, complete statements to make the resume represent you and just change the wording to your industry. **<u>You have what you need question solved.</u>**

> A. You will need several resumes for different types of jobs that highlight the qualities that the employer wants to see. If you're in financial services you will need a Branch Manager Resume that highlights your branch leadership, customer service and operational experience. You will also need a resume for Vice President of Branch operations that highlights your ability to manager leaders and strategic

thinking. You will also need another resume if you are also a lending manager or Vice President of Lending. In summary make a list of the positions you want and design a resume that highlights those skills. (Complete the Master Information Sheet in the Resume Folder)

B. What skills are employers looking for? Excellent question, go to the library or search the job descriptions on the internet (save the job descriptions in your Job Description Folder). If using paper folders, print out the skills, qualifications and file the printed information under specific job description tabs (you must stay organized) then design your resume stating your accomplishments and skills in each of these areas.

2. Cover Letter- This is a must. You must have several cover letters that address very specific accomplishments, equipment used and training. Your goal is to make the employer realize you have experience and skill depth that makes the decision maker want to know more about you.
   a. The cover letter is where you "Bragg" about your best accomplishments and why you are the person that will make this company better.

3. The Application Packet- We need to set up all information to make completing an application easy. This will pull together the majority of information you need for every application you complete. Complete the following documents in the Application Packet:
   a. The Job Application Employment Information Spread Sheet.
   b. Print and complete the Long Application Form. You will need your Start Date, End Date, Former Employer Name, Address, Email Address, etc.
   c. Complete the Application Questions. Our strategy is to answer the question

once and retain a copy so you are never rethinking the same question again and again. (For example, you may need a statement of your management philosophy, statement of how you handle conflict and a statement on why are you the best candidate for the job. But, let's not get caught up in the statements at this time let's keep moving.) We have entered often asked questions for you to answer in the "Application Folder under Application Questions".

4. References- Open your Reference Folder. The Reference spreadsheet allows you to formulate all needed reference information. This includes a list of several professional friends that will say good things about you. (See Folder-References and complete the "Reference Log"). Next, you want to tell the references what to say and make it easy for the references to help you so perform the following steps:

   a.   Call each reference to let them know you are looking for new employment and immediately ask them if they will be a reference and if you can share their contact information.

   b. Confirm the email, address and telephone numbers that you can distribute.

   c. Once they agree, inform them that you have a resume that you are sending them so they have a reference of your accomplishments. They will be relieved and now they are looking forward to saying good things about you and most of all they are prepared to help you. You just added an important element to your team. This is Your Team!!

d. Also tell them what job you are looking for and ask them to use their network and distribute your credentials to anyone that may have a job for you.

e. When you send them your resume and your cover letter as talking points tell them a "PERSONAL THANK YOU" and that you appreciate them helping you. Let them know you realize they did not have to help you but you are truly grateful for their support.

f. Finally, tell them to call you with any advice or potential leads. Let them know you will do the contacting and leg work for any referrals.

5. Job Description-Open your "Job Description Folder". This is the folder that will hold the Characteristics that make a successful employee for the position. You will have a job description for every job you want to apply for prior to applying for the job. (Store all Job Descriptions in the "Job Description Folder")

   a. Why? You want to research the wording that is used in the description and make sure your resume and cover letter uses the words, experience and skills that are being looked for in this specific employee, manager or executive. The skill set required for an assembler or bank teller is different from a Supervisor, Manager, Director or Vice President. This is our research folder of data we will use to build our resume.

Now let's go back to the Application Package Folder. You are ready to complete the "Long Job Employment Application". If we have done our work well you should have all the information at your fingertips.

III.   Let's Get Started

A.THE RESUME-Open the "Resume Folder":

"Open the "MASTER INFORMATION SHEET"-
Complete the Master Information Sheet-This document will organize your resume information so when you start writing the actual resume you have what you need at our finger tips:

Who do you want to be?
List 10 professional jobs you want. List the jobs in order of your first choice through your 10th choice. I mean, list the actual professional title of the position (Customer Service Representative, Vice President of _____, Director of _____, Manager of _____, Customer Relations Clerk, etc.) If you don't know the position title, this is the time to identify the proper job name –Who do you want to be in the future. I set out to be a Vice President of Lending, but I will settle for a Lending Manager, Loan Officer, Underwriter, Branch Manager, Vice President of Branch Operations, Customer Service Manager, etc.

- Now go to the internet, get a job description and skills needed to be successful .

-Do research on "What are the most important characteristics to be successful in this position"- The goal is to identify the 10 characteristics our "**BUZZ words** "that all Human Resource and Executives are looking for in a successful candidate. We are giving the resume the MEAT it needs to separate you from the rest of the file.

-Now we copy and paste this information as a job description for this position and title in our "Job Descriptions Folder".

1. Why are you the best choice?
    a. List your experience.
    b. List your accomplishments-What things did the company, department or organization accomplish that you consider impressive.
        i. Computer Conversion.
        ii. Merger with another company.
        iii. Increased Collection Staff.
        iv. Increased Customer Satisfaction from what to what

v. Increased Company Production from 1 thousand to 1 million.

vi. Implemented a new policy that reduced cost.

vii. Anything the company accomplished you have or had a hand in it.

viii. If you were fired, state what you learned and turn the negative event into a positive event. For example-You now place a high priority on being on time.

2. State 10 professional skills- Well organized, Manage accounting department, exceptional communicator, strategic thinker, team player, supportive, developed policy, operational manager, senior executive, developed branch operations, managed branch manager, superior advertising executive, develop advertising campaign, creative expert, customer relations expert, board member, etc.

3. Employment History (In the Application Packet-Complete the Former Job Information Sheet):

   a. Write down all employers from the most current to the oldest.

      i. Include the start date month, day and year to the ending date month, day and year. If currently employed state current employment.

      ii. State Company Name, Address, telephone number, Human Resources Contact or a boss that likes you contact information, telephone number, email address, Reason for leaving (i.e. I like career advancement).

         1. Do not list anyone who may say anything negative. It is better to say a company closed than to list a negative contact. Leave negative relationships where they belong in the past.

         2. If fired, just state your start and end date. If you state you were fired you will

probably not "GET A SECOND LOOK". Who wants to hire a problem or give a person they do not know an opportunity. Get the interview and then make the decision on what you want to share but "GET THE INTERVIEW"!!!

3. Legally your former company can be sued for telling negative personal information to anyone about you. So, don't open the door.

4. What special skills have you used:
    a. Opened the building daily-You have senior management security clearance.
    b. Manage 20 employees, Managed 5 managers and 19 loan Officers.
    c. Compliance Clearance and Training. State all Training and what you were certified or trained to do. For example, I went to and was certified in customer service or you have purchasing authority for $100,000.00.

d. Oversee all corporate correspondence-worked in the mail room making sure all documents are delivered to the proper department. It is all in the job explanation, be creative make sure you state your true worth.
   e. Implemented new dealer relationships
   f. Created new marketing plan that generated 6 new clients.

5. Computer training- in what areas? What is the name of the software you use at work for every day task- for example, Microsoft Word, Microsoft Excel, Galaxy, Symitar or ADP time clock. (Use the official product name/ industry product jargons?

6. Accomplishments:
   a. What did the company do that was amazing while you were on board?
   b. Did you increase performance rate customer service?
   c. Did the company have positive earning?
   d. Did the loan portfolio hit an all-time high due to your leadership and member relations strategy?

e. Did the customer account base increase?
f. Did you lower expenses?
g. Did you develop strategy to increase sales?

Be as specific in terms of dollars and cents as possible.

7. Education and License:
    a. List all official education stating with high school, college or special training where you achieved a certification.
    b. From newest to oldest-list the name of the institution, address, telephone number, start and end date, contact number, official certification. Make sure the name, address and telephone numbers are current and can be found on the internet.
    c. Also, include in career training "for example how to be a better executive, how to handle mean customers, who to motivate your team". Remember the training can be from previous employers, online courses, etc. If you have been trained to perform a specific

task, something that makes you more valuable than the competition, list it.

Now we are ready to pull this information together and use the Resume Master (In Resume Folder-Open Resume Format), just fill in the blanks with this information and you have your new resume. Remember you need to have a specific resume that highlights desired experience and accomplishments for each job you want to get.

1. **Make sure to NOT work on the "Resume Format":**
2. Open the "Resume Format"
    a. Save the Resume Format Under Another Name.
    b. Save AS "the New Resume1".
    c. You will have multiple resumes to fit each job and industry. If you have a different job you may need New Resume 2, 3 or 4.
    d. We want the resume to include the words and skills that we found in the job descriptions we stored in the job description folder (See Job Description Folder).

3. The "New Resume1" is ready for you just-**FILL IN THE BLANKS** we have made it easy!!

But, let's start off with one resume for the number one job you want to land. We don't want to waste time preparing for every situation because our GOAL is to get our number one choice.

WE NOW HAVE OUR NEW RESUME!!! TAKE A BREAK, YOU DESERVE IT GET A SNACK AND A DRINK. Now let's move on to the cover letter.

B.   COVER LETTER:

As we stated we will need a cover letter for every different job position. The cover letter is your BRAG sheet. Who are you, what have you done and why you are special? Finally, you are the choice that will solve the company's need. Now let's compose your cover letter:

First- Who are you, what do you want, why should I want you (i.e., what experience and skills do you offer).

Second-What have you accomplished, what is your professional mission and vision that the company needs.

Third-State special skills (i.e. what licensed do you have, notary, certified appraiser, licensed mortgage officer, speaking or presentation training, motivator or coach). We want your BEST SKILLS.

Finally, "The Close"-I look forward to speaking with (COMPANY NAME or CONTACT PERSONS NAME) about the (STATE THE SPECIFIC JOB or OPPORTUNITY). My contact number is

_____.

Sincerely,

Name
Telephone number again (we want to make it easy for the hiring person to contact you)

Now, as always **"I HAVE GOT YOU"**, use the example Cover letter in the Cover Letter Folder, change to your information and we are done.

1. **Make sure to NOT work on the "Sample Cover Letter"**:
2. Open the "Sample Cover Letter"
    1. Save the Cover Letter.
    2. Save AS " Cover Letter 1"
    3. You will have multiple cover letters to fit each job and industry. If you have a different job you may need Cover letter 2, 3 or 4.

CHECK MARK –"COVER LETTER 1" is ready for the number one job from your Master Information Spreadsheet which is stored in your Resume Folder.

At this point we have a Resume and Cover letter for a very specific position. The Resume should be saved in the Resume Folder and the Cover letter should be saved in the Cover letter Folder.

Now on to the References!

C. References:

We want to have 5 to 10 references. If you have references in the profession that are known and respected you MUST use them. What good are friends that do not support you!! This is no time for pride. Use the most impressive professionals with known, respected and recognized names. **Do not use anyone who you are not 100% positive will help you.**

Go to the reference spreadsheet which is stored in the Reference Folder. For each reference complete the requested information.

1. List the reference. State their name, address, contact number, email and professional position.
2. State how you know them. List professionals that are aware of your skills and have helped in the past. They are the ones that future employers will respect.
3. Call each reference. Get each references permission to use them as a reference. Tell them you are sending them your list of accomplishments and skills.

4. Once they accept to be a reference-confirm all of their contact information and that you have the best contact information to share.
5. Send an email of **appreciation thanking them** for being on your team and let them know that when they need help you are there for them.

Now we are ready!! We have our first future job resume, cover letter and references. WE HAVE OUR TOOLS AND WEAPONS TO START BATTLE, LET'S BEGIN.

IV. THE BATTLE BEGINS!!!!!!!
GETTING THE WORD OUT!!

Internet Job Search Set Up and Dangers:

First, we want to get the new technology and the Internet working for you. Then we will move to personal contacts, etc. In today's world all job opportunities worth anything are on the internet. Why? Because the internet opens up the World for Human Resource Departments to get the word out that they have a need and want to fill that need. From your perspective you have a need and want the world to know you can satisfy their needs.

The internet and job sites can put you immediately in the know with what jobs are available, the skills sets that are needed, where to send your information and often allow you to complete an application/apply for job.

Of all the web sites I used, many sites just refer you to other job sites and in summary they are a waste of time. You want job sites that have jobs you can apply for immediately or be taken to apply at the corporate job site.

DANGER: Let's discuss what to **AVOID** in completing **INTERNET Applications**:

1. Once you have uploaded the resume you must always verify that the information on the application is accurate. Take your time and slowly review the information. It must be accurate to get a great look from the Human Resource Manager.
2. Do not Skip any questions, the software will not allow you to move to the next page if information is missed.
3. When you get tired stop. Take a nap, workout or get a bite to eat. You must remember your application is your presentation to the company of your skill set.
4. Make sure you save your work at every turn. You never know when the company site or your computer system will stop working. If you SAVE, you can start again at your current spot. We are not wasting any energy being upset over lost work.
5. Often a corporate web site is where you are asked questions, "What is your management philosophy"? This is when you should save your work, go off site, name the question that is asked and then really write up a great

statement that you keep for future answers in the "Application" Folder, in the "Statement" Folder. Once you complete your answer SAVE IT as an "Application Question and Answer" word document (Make sure you name the word document "Answer to _____"). Now the next time this question is asked all you need to do is go to your "Statement" folder, Copy your previous write up and Paste on the application. This is how and why we will build our "Statement" folder.

1. Job Search Sites

I have my list of top job sites to use to get you in the know and get you your new job. Remember, you can set up multiple job searches for different positions from the same job search site but first let's just focus on our number 1 job choice.

***See the list of "Preferred Job Search Sites" in the Username/Password Folder.**

1. Indeed
   a. http://www.indeed.com/

2. Zip Recruiter
   a. https://www.ziprecruiter.com/

3. Career Builder
   a. http://www.careerbuilder.com/
   b. I recommend Career Builder because they allow you to apply for positions with a click of the apply button and they inform you if you already applied. I like sites that help me be professional.

4. Ladder
   a. http://www.theladders.com/
5. Monster
   a. http://www.monster.com/

A -Internet job search set up:

1. Open your "Username/Password" Folder
   a. Open the "Preferred Job Search Sites" Spreadsheet.
   b. Open your "Username/Password" Spreadsheet.
   c. Start your user name and password list for job sites.
      1. You will have several user name and password list. You will have one spreadsheet tab for internet job search sites, one for corporate sites, etc. (See Tabs at bottom of spreadsheet- Internet, Corporations and Other). This spreadsheet is your **"internet job search master control sheet"**. Make sure you take your time and list the user names and passwords correctly.
2. As soon as you set up a user name and password for an internet search site log all the way out.
     Then log in to make sure the new user name and passwords work. (There is nothing more frustrating than completing a profile and then not being able to get to the profile because your user name and password is not working. Take your time.)

3.   Upload your Cover letters, Resumes and references for **_"public display"_**. This is how we let employers that are searching for talent find your resume for review. This is also the process where you can click a button and your resume is immediately forwarded to the hiring manager.

B. Corporate Job Search Strategy

-If you see a position that you really want while reviewing the job search information complete the internet application process. ALSO, go to the company web site!

-At the company web site search for a "Career or Employment" Tab.

- Register with the employment web site, set up user name and log in (enter this information under the "Corporate Tab" on the Username Password Spreadsheet). Search for the position and officially fill out an application.

1. SETTING UP CORPORATE SEARCH ENGINE

The employment search is your best friend. The web site searches for jobs that meet your job description. You can set up multiple searches so be very specific.

> 1. List your job positions name: Lending, Vice President, Manager of Operations, Teller, File Clerk, Stock Handler, etc.
> 2. List the location where you want to work.
> 3. State any specific information because you don't want random positions.

4. List if you are willing to relocate.

5. The search will ask you how often you want to be notified, I recommend weekly. Set up to be notified by different sites or corporations on different day. Have the different sites set up to notify you each day of the week. This way you are not overwhelmed every day with all sites and miss an opportunity.

6.   You want to have results from one site on Monday, Tuesday, Wednesday, Thursday and Friday. (It is ok to delete a job site and reset the search engine if the information is not correct or you want to be notified on a different day, no biggie).

7. Now you can set up a job search for your second future job choice and third choice (This information in on your "Master Information Sheet" in your resume folder). Now you have your top 3 future positions being identified daily. What you will find is that the best web sites will allow you to see positions and just hit apply to send your cover letter and resume. You check the job searches daily for an hour or two and apply for all jobs

that you desire. This is how we maximize your job application process.

    a. See my list of "Preferred Sites Spreadsheet" in the Username/Password Folder.

8. Some sites will cost money. Always use or ask for the 30 day free trial. (I.e. Ladder, Monster-premium, Beyond, etc.). I did use these web sites and got some great opportunities.

    A.   Make sure you know a week ahead of time when the free enrollment period will end. If you do not cancel the service the monthly charge will be automatically charged to your debit or credit card.

    B. If you do not want to continue using the service you MUST cancel the service.

9. Do not waste your time applying for positions you are not qualified to perform. Maximize your emotional and physical energy.

C. Our Internet Strategy

1. Now you have used the internet job search venue to apply.
2. You have also, now officially applied on the corporate web site **which separates you from all the other internet candidates!**
3. Stay Aggressive. Also, see if you can find out the Human Resources Manager's name and email address. If possible send an email that states you applied via the internet, that you have completed the official company application and that you look forward to a conversation about this great opportunity.
4. Make sure you attach the cover letter, resume and reference. I often used my cover letter as the "email write up" addressed to the Human Resources V.P. or Manager. I want them to know I applied via the internet and have completed the corporate application. This action has just made the H.R. Executive's job a little easier and may just push you to the top of the candidate pile or at the very least they know you are smart and aggressive. A winner!!

V. Targeting-Getting the Word Out-Part II
1. How to Target Corporate Jobs and Opportunities:

2. List all companies that are in the industry where you have job experience and companies that need your talents.
   a. If you are not sure of the companies, go to the internet and enter "Top 30 companies in your INDUSTRY, CITY OR STATE".
   b. Once you have the list go to each corporation's web site.
3. Register on each of the corporate career web sites-WAIT!! Make sure you are on the actual corporate web site and not a job search site (which is a site that leads to other job sites).
   a. Under the Corporate Tab of your "User Name and Password Spreadsheet" enter the corporate name, user name and password of each corporate web site.
   b. Up load your cover letter, resume and references.
   c. Go to the search engine and put in your position.

d. Apply for all jobs that meet your skill set.

e. What is really great about most corporate applications is once you have entered information to complete an application for a specific job all other jobs within the same corporation will allow your applications to Pre-Fill with previously entered application information (This is a great time saver).

    i. Pre-Fill allows the information on the application to be used and you only have to answer Federal Hiring Questions which saves you the time of filling in the same information OVER and OVER again.

    ii. Make sure you apply for all jobs that fit your skill set don't get locked into your old position. Think of other positions for which that you have the skill set and apply for those positions also (i.e., if you were a customer service supervisor apply for the customer service manager).

4. Now set up your search engine for the corporation to notify you of all new jobs that fit your skill set. Make sure you enter Manager or Operation Area-Finance, Lending, etc.
    a. Now you will get updates and I would re-state that you only want a weekly update.

Repeat the process for every corporation you want to work with in the future.

5. DANGER: Let's discuss items to avoid in Corporate Pre-fills and Applications: (THIS IS SO IMPORTANT I SAID IT TWICE)

    a. Once you have uploaded the resume you must always verify that the information on the application is accurate. Take your time and slowly review the information it must be accurate to get a great look from the Human Resource Manager.
    b. Do not skip any questions, the software will not allow you to move to the next page if information is missed.
    c. When you get tired, stop. Take a nap, workout or get a bite to eat. You must

remember your application is your presentation to the company of your skill set.

d. Make sure you save your work at every turn. You never know when the company or your computer system will stop working. If you SAVE, you can start again at your current spot. We are not wasting any energy being upset over lost work.

e. Often a corporate web site is where you are asked questions- "What is your management philosophy"? This is when you should save your work, go off site, name the question that is asked and then really write up a great statement that you keep for future answers in the Application Packet Folder in the "Application Questions" word document. Now the next time this question is asked all you need to do is go to your folder of statements, Copy your previous write up and Paste on the next application. This is how and why we will build our statement folder.

Now we have our Internet Team Working, Our corporate Team Working and Next We Set Up our Local, State and Federal Team.

VI: Government Job-Getting the Word Out =Part III

A. How to start and what to do at Local, State and Federal Government Employment Web Sites:

The government has many jobs that must be filled in order to run a City, State, County and Country.

1. For a quick start, go to the "Username Password" Folder (Check out our "Preferred Job Site Spreadsheet" and click the "Government Tab" at the bottom of the spreadsheet).

2. To create your own search sites. Go to your search engine, type "employment for your city, state, county" and of course the "USA Jobs".

   a. Create a log-in and create a user name and password.

3. Now you are in the search engine, look for positions that need your skilled position. I often will enter "all full time jobs" just to see what is listed on the web site. But, if you are an accountant or bus driver enter your specific job. Don't waste this initial time. Be specific and move from city job site, to the

State, County and USA or Federal Government Careers or job website.

    a. The USA website is now called "USA careers".

4. Now set up your search criteria and get your weekly notifications.

5. Let's apply for jobs that come up under my new search engine.

    a. Remember if you apply for multiple jobs you will not have to fill out the same information over and over again.

    b. You normally just have to answer the Federal Fair Employment Questions and then submit.

6. When applying for government employment it is very important to read the qualifications. If you do not have the specific classification or qualifications DO NOT WASTE YOUR TIME. The government hiring practice must show the minimum skill and education requirements-make sure you review this information.

    a. Apply only where you can get the job!!

7. Set up search engines for every 2 weeks. The government jobs often have 30 or more days that a job must be posted.

VII: FINANCES

A. What to do immediately, second and third-You will make IT!!!

One of the most horrible parts of being unemployed is that you have no New money to pay for Old bills. But, **do not panic,** we have a step by step plan.

Part 1-The Basics

1. Apply for unemployment compensation-You normally can call in and apply over the telephone or over the internet.
    a. But remember the unemployment office is your friend and it is a "Great idea" to meet the government employees that work on helping citizens find jobs daily.
    b. Develop a relationship with the unemployment office staff so they know your contact information.
2. You must make a list of the expenses you have to pay and the income you have to use.
    a. First list all bills, including cable, medical, car notes, house notes/rent

payment, property taxes, utility bills and credit card bills.

b. Now list all income that you have at your disposal, future income, investments, 401K money/retirement money, life insurance policies with an investment feature, etc.

c. Determine if you have medical insurance to cover you and your family (i.e. COBRA or do you need Obama care). This is a major decision and you must have coverage because one illness can destroy ALL your cash flow options!!!!

3. Now you need to decide what expenses can be immediately cut.

   a. Luxury items, monthly club dues, premium cable channels and the weekly night out with the girls and boys may need to go.

4. Tell the family what WE need to do to move forward and how everyone can help. They need to know that you are stressed and that you need to be mentally and physically loved in this process.

   a. Tell the family on a need to know basis as adjustments to tighten the budget must be made to lower the overall emotional effect on the family.

b. They need to understand that you will not be going out to dinner every Friday or spending a 100.00 to buy the latest concert ticket.

5. Now let's match Total Available Income (A) verses Life Needs-Basics Shelter, Transportation, Utilities, Food, Clothing and Property Taxes (B). This is your remaining operating income /money(C).

a. After you subtract the (C) remaining operating income/money from the remaining unsecured expenses (i.e. credit cards, charge cards, etc.). You are left with a positive or negative number. A1. If you have a positive number you have operating income (remaining cash). If you have a negative number (you do not have enough cash to pay current obligations and live).

Part 2-Time Frame

1. For the first 30 to 60 days call all debtors and get due date extensions to stock pile cash.
   a. Car notes, mortgages, credit cards will normally give you one hardship extension.
   b. Make sure you know when you reach 25 days so you can pay without being hit with a 30 day late on your credit report which will lower your credit score.
   c. Look to consolidate all credit cards into long term personal loans while your credit score is high. The goal is to lower monthly personal outflow of cash to equal current cash on hand/current cash flow.
2. Now you have 30 to 60 days to secure new income to help with expenses. Now remember, if you have savings we want to limit using these funds.

3. Now if you have a ton of credit card debt that is taking all your cash flow. Consider paying off credit card debt with savings or retirement funds to lower the monthly out flow of cash.

   a. WHAT YOU DO NOT WANT TO DO IS KEEP USING RETIREMENT INCOME TO PAYOFF MONTHLY CREDIT CARD BILLS. EVERY DOLLAR OF RETIREMENT FUNDS THAT IS USED TO PAY A MONTHLY MINMUM CREDIT CARD PAYMENTIS A HUGEWASTE OF YOUR ASSETS/Cash money.

4. If you do not have enough income to pay for the major expenses and eliminate the credit card debts. Then Bankruptcy is a viable option.

   a. This may be a rare time in your life where your income is low enough to apply for bankruptcy and eliminate all credit card debt. Don't let your ego get in the way of this option. You can always rebuild your credit score.

   b. Now some professions are rated by the credit score and if you must file you need to tell future employers that due to your personal situation after being laid off you had to file to protect your assets and family.

    i. Just put it on the table so the information is not a surprise to a future employer. You might want to wait until you know you are a viable candidate.

    ii. Don't hurt your own cause without reason.

5. Now, let's get back to the debt consolidation. If you payoff credit cards with your retirement funds you MUST lower your debt load so you do not need to file bankruptcy.

    a. If you are paying off your credit card debt and it will not free you from debt then keep the protected retirement funds (bankruptcy WILL not touch the retirement money) and file.

    b. You will normally be able to keep your home, cars and other major life functioning assets.

6. If you use your retirement funds put aside the penalty you will have to pay on your

tax return. If you use $10,000.00 you will normally have a $3,000.00 penalty to pay on your taxes. So, make sure the $7,000.00 you use is really making you able to function (INCREASE CURRENT MONTHLY CASH FLOW) on current cash flow.

7. I also recommend contacting a credit counselor that is **free** and see if they can help you identify financial options for your family. They may be able to help you lower your monthly expenses and enable your income to cover your expenses.

8. If you can unload $80,000.00 in credit card debt call it a day and file BK.

Part 3-How to handle your Family, Friends and Lovers

Your family loves you and you love them. The family needs to all know we are in a fight and we will WIN!! But, we have to make some sacrifices. The family will be sad **as you are** but they will start to work with you as they see you are fighting to move forward. This is also a great example that your children will remember when life hurts them, to not give up, but to dig in and fight to be successful. They will appreciate seeing you up at 7:00 AM applying for new jobs, checking your search engines and making contacts for your new adventure every day.

Do not hide, tell all friends, contacts and associates that you are on the job market so they can all be supportive and help you!! Remember the **number one goal** is to get **employed** and we have no time for negative thoughts, pride or self-doubt. Whatever it is, you have to deal with the future, learn from the past but don't waste energy wondering why!! We are wondering what the next great opportunity will be?

Bottom line is you are on one of life's great adventures. Your reaction will show your courage and strength you never knew you had in your character. On days when you want to just cry and be mad at GOD just get up and go to work!! Cry, dry your tears, get mad and FIGHT! Fight even if it is just sending out one resume or applying for one job that day. You still moved forward by a baby step and you will be proud of yourself at the end of the day.

Your lover, this is a person that is worried about you, your life together and your relationship. DON'T ISOLATE THEM AND DO NOT HIDE THE FACT THAT YOU AREIN ONE OF THE BIGGEST BATTLES OF YOUR LIFE! This is the time you really need your support base. Let them know your financial plan and get their support. If they will not support you then you need to not look to them for support and GO FOR IT YOURSELF, IT IS UP TO YOU TO MAKE THIS NEW OPPORTUNITY HAPPEN. But, hopefully you are blessed to have someone who truly loves you. If they truly love you then they will be with you in good times and bad times. I hope you have a wife like I do. She was mad that the situation had taken place but she also loved me enough to know whatever caused the loss of work I WAS A VICTIM AND WE HAVE TO LOVE AND WORK TO GET PASS THIS CHALLENGE! But remember your loved one is in pain also. You have placed both of you in a situation of stress. It is about both of you and your life. So, your significant other deserves to know and be up to date on what you're doing every step of the way. This will reinforce your efforts and give your significant other courage to move forward with you.

Your significant other may or may not be a good sounding board. They will want to know what happen and they deserve the truth. They deserve the opportunity to be sad and disappointed!! It is not only about you, it is about US! So, identify what is the best way to interact with your best friend of life.

1. **GIVE THIS TO YOUR SIGNIFICANT OTHER, FROM ME:**

As an employed and successful person that has been unemployed understand that as long as you support your lover this will pass. But, you must support your lover! He or she is hurt emotionally, spiritually, financially and physically! In summary, they are in bad shape. As their best friend and PARTNER, YOU NEED TO LET THEM KNOW THAT YOU WILL HELP THEM AND YOU BELIEVE IN THEM. Even if they were wrong and contributed to losing their job, it does not matter. We are moving forward, we will learn from the past and our best days are in the future.

3a. How do you help:

Tell them you "Love them" and that you are there to support them in whatever they need to do to move forward. LISTEN TO THEIR PLAN AND SUPPORT THEIR STRATEGY! Make sure they go for walks, laugh and stay is a positive mental and physical state of mind. Let them know your love transcends life's challenges. If you catch them praying or crying, pray with them or cry with them. Then together in love move forward. This experience can be one of life's gifts to your relationship, giving you both the opportunity to understand the words "FOR BETTER OR WORSE", show you are an inseparable team.

Also, help make hard financial decisions by not spending for unnecessary expenses. Remember you both are in a battle and together you will win. Cut out the expensive dinners and dates. Only spend for necessities until the income is flowing in and not out. These are very hard situations, so in love show that what matters in you, your significant other and your children. No one else's perspective matters!

Remember I love you and thank you for your support! I could not have made it without my loving wife. She showed me what a strong supporter means and how much she loves me! I was lucky I had my GOD, my wife and my wonderful family!! My entire support team was working, praying and being supportive. Be there for your lover!!

Part 4-Physical!!!!

<u>Your body, keep it in a good state, it helps you mentally!</u>

You are physically exhausted, your stress level is high and your body is tired due to having to get a job to support yourself and possibly your family. You are right, this is horrible but we have the plan to help you make it and be successful. You have to start working out to let the body help the brain. Your workout can be walking, running, video workouts for cardio and body toning. Go for it, start at 30 minutes, then eat (light meals nothing to make you tired or sleepy) and get started finding the next job. This is a daily routine. Remember you can also use the workout as the day ending activity as a reward. But, for me I needed the morning workout to shake off any negative mental demons and start me on a positive mental daily routine. You know we are going forward and looking for GREATNESS!!

You must eat breakfast, lunch and dinner to stay strong. Don't over eat because you need to stay alert to complete our daily work. Check in with your doctor and explain your stress. You may need some help sleeping due to you being mentally sad and worried about tomorrow. Make sure you are taking vitamins and you may need a relaxer at night to help you sleep. You need to sleep, if you are waking up and sad at night this is normal. Remember you are dealing with sadness and depression. You may just need to rest more, you must forget the past/forgive the bad people who hurt you, **<u>forgive yourself</u>**, forgive yourself (I said it twice, because I am my worst critic, I had to forgive me for any short comings, use it as a lesson for the future and move to GREATNESS. IN MY FAITH, GOD WAS DEVELOPING ME FOR MY FUTURE GREATNESS!! NOW I HAVE TO GO AND GET IT) and move on- this is your LIFE live it! The past does not own you and your happiness-YOU DO!

If you have a dream project and have not been able to do it because of your past job or working, do it! Go for an early morning walk in the summer-enjoy the freedom, pick up your kids from school and walk them home or go to your children's school basketball game. Do not just waste this time being hard on yourself. Stay organized, work your job plan, enjoy the freedom (as long as you get in 8 hours of work Monday –

Friday, looking for the job), enjoy the other 16 hours with rest and family. If you have a lap-top computer and can work outside on the porch or deck-DO IT!!! While working inside your home-turn on the radio or television to listen to music or game shows. Anything that allows you to have a great environment while achieving your goal of getting the job. When you make the environment depressing it is draining your energy and soul. Listen to positive music, positive movies or shows that are inspirational and motivating. Remember it is "OK" to be happy as you create to find the next job and the next great opportunity. You are a Conqueror!! You are FIGHTING and enjoying life!

Remember! Do not listen to sad news, depressing shows or anything negative. You must have all your filters working toward happiness, comedy, love and success! This is how you will win and BE BLESSED with the next GREAT JOB or idea that will fulfill your life.

I Believe in YOU!

Remember, I love you; we are going to find the next step in your life. You take the next job that starts to generate new income but if it is not the job that is paying you what you are worth **keep working the job plan.** Any opportunity that generates new income "take it" and give it your best effort while searching for the job you're worth! These efforts keep your skills sharp and the energy around you stays positives as you continue to drive your success!! When you get the job or opportunity of your dreams it is not time to relax but time to perform. BE YOU, BE GREAT, AND DON'T FORGET TOWRITE ME. I WANT TO HERE ABOUT YOUR JOURNEY AND ADVENTURE!

In Love,
Lee A. Bailey

Finished on November 1, 2015 the day my first nephew died Eddie Michael Bailey. What a day and what a life I am living. I am blessed to have known you my dearest nephew and I will miss you so!! May you RIP and GOD take care of the family! Now, helping "YOU" is what makes this day positive-Let's get this career and job!

Supporting Documents

All ready to use Word documents and Excel spreadsheets can be purchased at winner@lemonsqueezebc.com for $15.00

MENTAL REPAIR: Answer and clear your mind

Why do I need a Job:

What did I do?

Why am I in this situation?

Who caused me the problems?

What did I do that caused this to happen?

Who mistreated me and who did I mistreat?

Who must I forgive to move forward?

Now what do I need to do to enable myself to move forward?

What is my motivation to fight to move forward?

Now I am moving forward there is nothing else to do?

Resume and Documentation Folder:
MASTER
INFORMATION SHEET-
Develop an Excel Spreadsheet
and list each topic as a "Row":

WHAT DO YOU WANT TO BE:
LIST THE TOP 10 POSITIONS WITH THE PROPER JOB DESCRIPTON:

1
2
3
4
5
6
7
8
9
10

WHY ARE YOU THE BEST CHOICE FOR THESE POSITIONS:

List Experience   List Accomplishments

State your top 10 skills

List all Employers

Master
Continue:

What Skills have you used in your day to day work experience?

What computer training do you have state all systems and software used?

Professional Accomplishments?

List all Educational Institutions?
Start Date   End Date   Degree   Major

Other Education?

Type of Course and learned skill or certification

Resume Folder:

Name
Street Address, City, State Zip Code
Contract Telephone Number (m), Contact Email Address

Position Title (Manger of Consumer Relations or Salesman)

(YOUR NAME) is a proven **(WHO IS YOU OR WHAT EXPERIENCE)** in the fast-paced and intricate realm of **(What Industry)**. This includes delivering **(What did you do exceptionally well)**. Excellent oral and written communication skills, with a proven track record of providing **(What?** Example-New business development expert, valued for coaching and mentoring skills)**. *Areas of expertise and professional strengths include:*

• List what positions you have held?	• What management skills?	• What projects have you completed?
• Example- Regional Sales Manager	• Example- Executive Board Presentations	• Example: Sales manager or assembly worker
• Example: Managed Student Corporate and Government Regulatory Relations	• Example: Network well with others	• Example: Develop New Business

CAREER ACCOMPLISHMENTS

- State positive things you have done or contributed
- Example: Successfully lend, underwrite, developed and managed branch, corporate operations and sales finance team
- Example: Worked 6 years with outstanding performance evaluations Appointed COO of Consumer Lending and Operations, SVP of Lending, Collections and Operations, SVP of Commercial Lending and Business Development (Auto, Unsecured, Secured, Credit Card and Commercial Lending).
- What have you done well –State title that companies will know
- What have you done well-State functions that companies will know

- What have you done well-State what positions you have help in organizations
- What have you done well-State personal accomplishments
- Increased Sales Finance loans from $4,680,000 to $22,500,000 yearly.
- State Awards you have received: Business Magazine Selected Business Executive of the Year for 40 Under 40

EDUCATION/CERTIFICATIONS

List the Degree you received, year received
University/School Name
City, State

List all training you have received to make you valuable to an employer-4 Maximum
List Training that makes an employer know you are special and have special skills
List if you are a leader-Example: Junior Achievement Counselor

Resume Continue:

PROFESSIONAL EXPERIENCE

Where are you currently working or last worked-Starting Month, Year to Last Day Worked or current employment: Official Job Title

- What did you do daily?
- Did you do anything to make the business better?
- What were you in charge of doing?
- .
- .
- .
- .

Where are you currently working or last worked-Starting Month, Year to Last Day Worked or current employment:

Official Job Title

- What did you do daily?
- Did you do anything to make the business better?
- What were you in charge of doing?
- .
- .
- .
- .

Where are you currently working or last worked-Starting Month, Year to Last Day Worked or current employment: Official Job Title

- What did you do daily?
- Did you do anything to make the business better?
- What were you in charge of doing?

Cover Letter Folder:

Dear (Contact Name is best or Human Resources Department) of (Company Name):

My name is Your Name. (Who are you?) I am an experienced financial services executive and strategic thinker who has held positions from Vice President of Regional Branch Operations (Michigan, Ohio, Indiana, New Jersey and Texas) to Membership and Lending Management. Under my leadership organizations have delivered exceptional member service that increased membership and loan portfolio growth. I have implemented strategies that have deepened the members' credit union connection which made us their primary financial institution.

(What's make your special for this Job) Example: Member connection and lifetime relationships (i.e. always being committed to improving members' superior product well-being and giving back to the community) are my top priority, and I expect every team member to work every day to earn the member's trust. I realize that we exist in a competitive (state the industry) environment and you must win the customer connection battle to be successful. (What makes you special?) I have many health care personal relationships that will enable me to build our connection with Yellow Fin. I have I have experience at successfully growing credit union membership, loan portfolios and I will successfully incorporate (State Process) into the culture of (State Company Name).

My attached resume, references and management philosophy write up supports my background and experience as a trusted executive leader in the financial services industry. My goal is to (what do you plan to do at your new job) that will stimulate member, product and loan portfolio growth. As you will read, I have been trained in (What do you know). I have over (years and/or educational experience/summarize your resume) that will make me an exceptional addition to your team.

I look forward to speaking with you and I am ready to start this exciting opportunity as your (restate the position).

Sincerely,

State your SUPERSTAR NAME
Best contact number
Best email address

Application Folder: This is your quick reference sheet
These are answers you copy and paste on other job applications:

What is makes you an excellent employee? What skills do they possess?

What is your idea of an excellent manager? What skills do they possess?

What skills do you possess that will make you successful in this position:

What types of measuring systems have you used to evaluate service levels?

If you are in charge of a sales team what do you do to maximize their performance? What if they are not meeting production goals? Describe the steps you would take to deal with the issue?

What method do you use to develop an organization? How do you train new and experience employees?

What is your management philosophy? How do you get everyone on the same page-management and non management members? What do you do when these two factions are in a disagreement?

What do you see as future challenges facing your industry? What would you do to prepare yourself and the company to function exceptionally in this environment?

Who was your worse employer and why?

Why did you leave your last job? What were your responsibilities and did you have any leadership responsibilities? Have you ever been a leader? If so where and what did you do to make the organization successful?

Complete the Job Application Employment Information- Set Up as an Excel Spread Sheet:

This will pull together the majority of information you need for every application you complete. You will need to title a column for each of these categories on the spreadsheet:

Company Name-All contact information:
Start Date:
End Date:
Former Employer Name:
Address:
City:
State:

Zip code:

Company contact number:

Former managers name (only state if Manager will say positive information):

Reason for leaving(I state "Career Advancement"):

Former Job Title:

Former Job Responsibilities-(State Important work performed, all leadership activity and computer activity):

Accomplishments you completed while employed-(brag if the company had profit increases say it):

Reference Sheet Folder: Set up the contact information for every reference you will use. Develop an Excel Spreadsheet and give each "Row" the following title:

Date Contacted:
Information Verified: Yes or No
Forwarded Resume and Talking Points: Yes or No
Name:
Address:
Contact Number
Email Address:
Relationship:
Length of time known:
Title:

Date Contacted:
Information Verified: Yes or No
Forwarded Resume and Talking Points: Yes or No
Name:
Address:
Contact Number:
Email Address:
Relationship:
Length of time known:
Title:

Team List-Who is on your team:

You will need to have 4 team lists. Use an
Excel Spreadsheet and make a tab for each team list:

Family
Friends
Network of Professional Contacts
Other contacts-anyone not listed above

Under each tab list the following columns:
<u>WHO IS ON YOUR TEAM</u>
   Name:
   Contact Number:
   Contact Date:
   Email Address:
   Address:
   Relationship:
   Length of Time Know:
   Title:
   What can they offer to help secure your next job:
   Forwarded Resume and Talking Points:

USER NAME AND PASSWORD FOLDER
List all web site employment contact information:

You will need to have 4 Username and Password tabs
 on the Excel Spreadsheet or Folders:

Internet Job Sites
Corporate Job Sites
Government Job Sites
Preferred Job Search Sites

Each Tab will have the following Columns:

Site Name
Internet Address
User Name
Password
Search Name

**Make sure you "IMMEDIATELY" write down
your user name and password.**
This is your internet team that will organize
 your daily work flow!
This is very important!

Hot Leads Folder:
 Excel spreadsheet includes columns:

Company Name

Company Web Site

Position

Position Description Reviewed

Company past and present history reviewed

New Company activity

Next Step (Are you sending your information directly to the hiring manager, department manager or VP
 of the area- Be Aggressive.

Interview Date

Contact Person

Company or Interview Address

Telephone Number of contact person

Email Address of Contact person

Date Thank you letter sent

Follow up date

Job Description Folder and Documentation:
This is the file where you keep all information
you print or read about your new position. I have
a folder set up on my computer for interesting
information I develop a **"WORD DOCUMENT"**
that I label with the job description.
Also, paste all information and links to specific
Information of interest.

List the "Job Description" for your new position/job:

**State or copy all important information on the
company, employer-** (I always review the
annual reports if available) **and the person who will
interview you:**

Salary Information:

Industry Information:

Hot News in the Industry:

**Company Address, web site, email and contact
information:**

ALL OF THE ABOVE DOCUMENTS AND SPREADSHEETS ARE READY ONLINE -DOWN LOAD!!

EMAIL ME AT:

WINNER@LEMONSQUEEZEBC.COM

$15.00-IS THE COST AND THE BEST MONEY YOU HAVE EVER INVESTED IN YOUR SUCCESS!

As you know, time is money, so eliminate Document and Spreadsheet set up time.